MW00531977

BEAUTYBERRY

Text & cover design by Heidi Reszies

Library of Congress Cataloging-in-Publication Data

Names: Donish, Cassie, 1982- author.
Title: Beautyberry / Cassie Donish.
Description: Northampton, MA : Slope Editions, [2018]
Identifiers: LCCN 2018044444 | ISBN 9780988522190 (pbk.)
Classification: LCC PS3604.O548 A6 2018 | DDC 811/.6--dc23
LC record available at https://lccn.loc.gov/2018044444

SLOPE EDITIONS

BEAUTYBERRY

CASSIE DONISH

for my mother,

Sheila Munsey

Thus desire
Becomes knowledge
Whether one loves
The world or loves
Shelter
From it

GEORGE OPPEN

This plant is very tolerant of fire.

USDA PLANTS DATABASE
Callicarpa americana

I CAME INTO THE WORLD

I came into the world
with a phenomenology
                in my hand
unable to distinguish
an ending from a beginning
and words were songs were
acts were light
were dreams were needs
                    were hunger
some years later
I went to the adult
novelties shop
by this time I had
tools to discern
act from thing from
self from world
body from time from pleasure
I knew exactly what it meant
                         to choose
so made love to a thousand wolves
with complete abandon
reckless but with
                solidarity
I had a hundred pups
and a nipple for each
but in a California river
I saw three generations
of my cowboy ancestors
had all fallen in
I had to carry
my ancestors around
in my clothes

I saw that my dream
had ended and the world
wasn't with us
though my poet friends know
how to carry objects
around in their pockets
that despite their mass
make walking
lighter: pale golden
apples, roses made of
confetti, invisible river
water, whiffs of song
some of my friends are
becoming more
religious and some
less
I sit in the back of the theater
on the floor
eating red candies
with five blond children
I imagine them asking
me why the world's
turned out this way
why every map
they've seen of the world
is a labyrinth of human
borders
go out into the small
bright day they'd tell me
and bring those you love back
to the places you've been loved
fail at naming us
as if only the truth
were metaphorical

SYMPOSIUM

on the morning of day two
I quivered where I'd fallen

beneath a green curtain
lit against the glass

on day three he wandered
and lit concentric paths

with soft eyes

and the syntax
of rabbits—let's stick

to the beautiful

what part is *not physical*?
what part can't be listed

with an eager mouth?

what's between an object's
name and its attributes

is the object—and yet

is a face made of features?
is *his face* even physical?

I can't decide

if I wish to leave my desire
in this world or take it with me

SUMMIT

to pour

into one another's line of

vision an image: stockings,

say: father,
friend, phone, leather
glove, siphon
this night

in which I approach

the edge of
the ravine where the
train stopped

it recoils with each
account or does it
advance

this blue night cut
out of water, dirty
humid light, scissor
it up, serve it here
we'll taste
everything
together

~

I allow the easy
sliding away from
one color

into a flower of sheets
knowing I said
otherwise, said I
don't allow only
to hear the sound
of it, to call
it untrue

one way to mislead
is to stay in one place
while everyone else
keeps walking

~

where is the pink
bed of water
whence came
this dark

you wake (I wake)
and any other
coincident thing, any

final thread leads back
to a lit
pool, greened

by undertow
pink tones inflecting
this as a body

~

I opened my mouth to taste the world
the final sweet preserves of a given
in which we stand in the kitchen
opening every
empty jar

I dive in you dive
up I dive through
the green ring

and slide
again toward
a mirror so dark, I can't
see anything

body of a white woman
sky hinged to a door
waiting for fallout

my hair
                    yesterday's
fire   caught

in a disaster or was the earthquake—no

no earthquake lasts that long

~

I only felt
you leave as trembling

I only love
to be a haunting

I consider any verge
a haunting

THE CALDERA

it wasn't a theater it wasn't
a season of leather
when we watched that crater
crack   its fractures blooming
                         black   lace
your skull your eyebrows your
famous desire your pierced
          and piercing   gaze
I asked you to trade me a story
that was the origin
          of hours   of detriment
O sweep me up you mad barking
seal of encounters
but not before I ship
my breasts to your anxious hands
your sheets your hunger your
                    consequent splendor
the world is dying I said
I don't believe that you said
you salmon you mare you
father of a wolf
your touch is what remained
when all your
          features   changed
your writhing made you
frail hollowed you out
                    made you proud
our debate will hold
the world in its mouth

A SIMMERING

I've come back from abroad he said
and all I want's
a margarita
so we sat at an outdoor table
on the sidewalk
at the end of summer
unfolding each word
like a feared diagnosis
I apologized, he wished
I'd said something
else, and vice versa
I asked if I
could squeeze lime
on the flesh
where his palm
meets his wrist
fine, he said
pressing a nickel
through his scars
he wanted to throw
the shining truck
across the restaurant
I became enfolded
in an unintelligible series
of decisions and retreats
from those decisions
and to decide
was like trying to distinguish
the color of an oak's leaves
at various times of day
and from various angles
and at night not seeing the tree at all

THE EXHIBITION

there are exceptions
to life's calamity
but no I am not one

I wear the moment
                                        of flesh in my flesh
in order to hunger
I familiar my order

and what if what I've looked for—

                                            yes, I think so now

at the opening
we stood beneath
huge paintings of   the sea

                              there was twill in the reeds
                              his beautiful girls
                              waved as they passed

I'll start referring to him
as my research

as being flared up

for enjoy
for heaven-sent

a warm day in which
blood in the throat

(I do feel afraid
when I see him)

(but is this only true

to a degree?)

I called myself habitual
an irrevocable

crossing

my habitual
an irrevocable crossing

everything still and
opening the field's
dirt the field's
fire (he squeezed my
hand)

I burn
the feed   the rain

steams me out

I did research on
the fundamentally flawed
air that cannot
measure itself

the pink outside
these tallest buildings
implies not heaviness
of sky

but the terror
of candied clouds
crushed into a box

his barrel of hail

his insides of rot

his sachet of violets

under the surface
were more surfaces

empty trough filled with leaves
we climbed the fence

passed each other over
passed our voices through

    fence like water
    leaves like water

                        but what can this not be said of

but then if I'm not speaking to—

what does, then, flow

if we could make choices

how one makes a bed

there's a way leaves have
when the music blares
and night sweeps up
                the visible
clanking fragments

      I walk down the middle
of a city street
past homes of cardboard
boarded up houses
perfect beds behind
            glass, lit in their
      department store
displays, women passed out
in cars, hope someone
will protect them

the rain's just

                        beyond that sign

I was flared up, that's
how I'll now refer
to his being
in the room

thus, morning

unfoundable

I could touch his wrist again
under the table made
of metal
water like you

what's so wrong with—

what's like light—

fainting
flared up
rain crouched

behind a sign

swaggery morning
drag it out like a sheet out
of a lake
last night

he dropped and broke
ceramic grapes and
ceramic light bulbs
my sister made
for an exhibit
          years before
                    we knew she was sick

I stand next to a tub
full of light bulbs
and other broken
shells

and in them glows
my flesh my flesh
has never been
so entirely
unbeheld

shaking out of the world

a trill

at the party
his body was
still the same
(grapes) as
before

fine: desire's

a manner
of speaking

his is graped
to the core
his presence
an uninterrupted offer

(continuously turning
down calm the way

one turns   down a bed)

but what is considered
our experience?

but is experience
your only thought?

the opening's
an event
in which the eyes
marshal the shine
of their old stage presence

the opening's
an event
I wade through

the gazebo's
become a force
field suctioned, so the
inner circle, so the sound
of it, so I

can't move

so give in ever
to anticipation's
lifelike body

the room
the beacon
the painted sea

was right where I stood
in flawed, dissolving
air, I whipped

up sound, I whipped
up song, I whittled
the song and hoped

they'd hold it
fast, hoped
it'd make

something shake

his mouth began
to fade but not
its color: it's just
beyond that sign

he flashed through me
I didn't want to but kept
washing the water
(his body)

how's this distance
for a life
I keep my distance
in an empty coin purse
until he leaves
it up to me

(I want these rooms

to flare against

their windows)

will I reach
the other side
if I keep walking

until bricks
smeared in sun
if I keep walking

until the body
the bluest regions
of the canvas

until I say
a word like
tapestretic

until the distance
between my fear
and the sound of it

opens and I
sliding down
slip through

NEW THEORY

my new theory is to make a boundary
between myself and the theory

then, between me and the boundary
to let a clouded region billow in, but to let
its shape be distinct: his face—

though the fog's blood-filled
when I return, and I'd best
have a line for it

though I can tell the fog's all upshot
though I admit it's its mug I'm
holding out the window

to let a contained song bask
at the edges of the tract
but if it grow perceptible

to be emboldened to rein it in

the dusk has always been a horse in its own light

THE SESSION

you are in fact
the architect
of the labyrinth
through which you wander
devastatedly
said the man
in his basement studio
when I pointed at
my bee-stung lip
as I lay on the floor
waiting for him
to massage the truth
upward from my belly
so it would, rising,
escape into the walls
of purple jacaranda
blossoms
and into the street
where children ate
fat tortas
and jumped through
ancient, fountainous
trees of stone
while brass instruments
sucked out the living
breath of men on every
corner—I lisped (not
in my usual manner) through
my swollen face
and winced and insisted:
a place has so much

grace to offer, but what
if a pack of wild
city dogs hunts me
down, tears me up each
night on the way
home from our friend's
performances
on the cognitive dreamery
of birds, the theater
where each night I long
to press my lips
to your cheeky
linguistic sensibilities?
what if all the time
I carry honey in my
pockets, disguising
a wound?
what if I still see
only tiny round
green leaves fluttering
in and out of loud
nearly deathening
patterns, yet know
this is no substitute
for things to say
in real conversation—well,
he exclaimed, once,
before this life
I was a traveling
craftsman, a carpenter,
I wore tall black
boots and hat and walked
the German countryside,
families took

me in, that's the
tradition, and now
I'm entranced with
basements and the void
and I don't need a
license for that
and I drink mezcal in
bars where son jarocho
bands stomp
the music of our blood
and I'll never leave
Mexico even if I
leave Mexico, not unless
I go to Italy,
understand? I don't
even care if I talk
through entire American
movies, I play only
American boardgames
on rooftops and only
with the moon
when it's low enough,
get it? I need you to cry
from your stomach now,
okay? I need you
to breathe
into where my fist's
displacing your
abdominal
muscles, to speak
as if you know
my hands are folded
in your lungs

UNDER THE EAVES

you should know by now that I experience my skin
as tiny pinpricks emitting soft refracted light

rendering a desirable
world

what I say has a lie in it
still speaking, I've returned from the meadow
from the pillowed queen anne's
lace, yarrow, excess, lupine by the roadside draining
oils upward into a pierced blue
and it's not that you flash through me
but between any two objects
is a vibrating that determines an impulse
the pulse of the exchange—

here, have a piece of glowing candy
take it as a truce

SOLILOQUY

cutting through the outskirts
of a picnic a soccer game
hearing the fragments
                    as others walk by
and I tried to explain, to tell him I wasn't—
a stream under the rose mallow
the cicadas are rising and falling fears
those red berries are poisonous and
                              you too will suffer
I've been afraid
of pain though I've mostly
been healthy surrounded
by others with illness
and as I pass parked cars
I worry that inside one of them
a man is threatening a woman
                                        a hand
on her wrist as people
walk with their cell phones
close to their mouths
towards fountains and pavilions
the busts of composers
on pillars the blue canopy
                              of a birthday
dogs with and without leashes
dogs with and without balls
ducks with and without mothers
flowers with and without names I
know and I wish to saturate your
vision with colors that don't
represent anything but
                        themselves I see

two girls walking they can't be
more than twelve my lover keeps
telling me about crimes
in this city comma period
comma period period
a willow a chirp an engine as
the hour rinses the outlines
                                        of the leaves

EVERY BODY WANTS TO REVEAL ITS HISTORY

the years were shot through
with flying and tangled cords of light
which I parted and swimming out
into the dark deserted cove

I watched my mother
as she'd watched hers
who'd watched hers and this
is a long maternal line of rifts
with fathers husbands
lovers

the body wants
to open and spill its history
its history's all shuttered up in skin

my Irish blood's
patterned tides beneath pale skin
and pale eyes my casual pallor

the body wants to step outside
of the body so I step into you
evening air or presence of
an almost intimacy

did I tell you how when my father died
a voice awoke inside my blood
it was an anxious sound a Yiddish song
of agitated birds departing from mythical red trees
O wild prayer of coalescing waters
have I been wrong in every moment
does the body want to fasten shut
and hide its ruptures its raptures
its nearness to the gate

HUMAN KNOWLEDGE

all around us, society is being used
to tell itself a story.

Know what it doesn't say?

Doesn't say precisely how
this one brick got here, how it got
to be part of this walkway, only one
of its faces visible.

Doesn't say how this brick shines
with wind. *You're beautiful.*

One thing I'm not debating
with myself is whether
the desire to say so
is urgent.

Know what we are?

Two animals that crossed paths.

Know why I didn't speak?

Trying to hush
the moan I heard
in my head.

I'm in pain from the pleasure
of pressure. Body wishing
this little moment
(the sun just set, the sky dim,
water sloshing against brick)
could be its last

scattered across a gameboard,
twelve small rooms,
each with its own coordinates,
a minimum of four dimensions.

Look into the first room.
An apartment on a hill, in spring,
some friends are listening to a record
and eating eggs.

Stand with me
on any square of kitchen,
dance with me there
on the cold tile.

Be slow about it. Be killing
with your time

I can't hear what you're asking,

maybe you're not
saying anything.

I answer that your skin smells like
lemon, and when we're in the fields
the scent gets stronger,

and when I speak
your skin sloughs off
and yellow light shoots from the top
of your head into the sky.

Much later, we'll all be
just little hills
with stones on top.
I have a sweet feeling

look in this window.
A banquet
is being held
in a long hallway.
You're the one
on the table
on all fours
with plump cherries
stuffing your mouth.
I move around you in circles
with the others,
playing a version
of musical chairs.
Why wouldn't I want
to tell a story?
This is a dirty
scene in it.
When the music
stops, we all
rush toward you,
we all fall down

if the universe is an overgrown garden
the size of a universe—

and if all human knowledge is the size
of this little lemon balm patch

my body sends information to
my body. Out with it.

The sky, too, has a soul.

Above a cloud field,
the light keeps painting
a pink sea, a rosy welt.

Your cheeks, too, are pinked.

You're in motion
because beheld

dreamed I put my throat
in your throat and sang.

Then fog entered the city.
No one could tell who was who.
You grabbed me and struck your match,
one letter in the white cloud.

When I saw you again
(wake up

you
cathedral)

I put my throat
in your throat,

lit you from within—
one kind of ghost

I took a street,
I put my palm over its eye.
But the street led to a shore;
but when the ocean splashed out,
there was a water stain on the sky in the shape of a vertebra.

My body was a sculpture made only of salt. It fell beneath
a curtain, the interminable salt water
parting

BEAUTYBERRY

*

Many seasons after we became lovers, we started to get a system down. Before this, the years had often been tragic with distraction. Our encounters were inconsistent, near paradox.

What was recognizable, and good, was silence. Once we saw this, the system was in view. We'd meet in a city that was new to both of us. We'd meet in the hotel bar. I'd wear my pearls. We'd talk for a while, say what was new. My knees pressed together between yours, your hands on my thighs. Your trembling made me tremble.

I should say that this is the way things used to begin sometimes too, before the system. This trembling in the first hours. But before the system, it would continue all night, become violent. One of us might rip the other apart once we were alone. It was always by accident. It must've been because of the talking. Somehow we learned this, though of course, we never spoke of it.

*

With the system, we'd let the talking and trembling go on, but there was a boundary.

As we moved through the long hallway, our voices would start to sound distant, floating all around us, coming from anywhere.

*

It's hard for me to imagine what might be heard or understood if one were to listen to our last bits of speech before crossing the threshold.

> *the rain had to carry us home*
>
> *why wouldn't one replace a birdbath with falling stars, just in case*

I believe now that the approaching silence was pressed against us from within the room, from the other side of the door, and before that door even opened, the silence had begun to gesture in our direction with such force that it pushed our usual sense of agency out the backs of our heads.

I would never say this to you. Occasionally I do worry I've made too many agreements, but at this point, the system is in place.

*

I've accomplished little. I'm preoccupied with what may come, when I might next hear those fragments, which I forget but reinvent.

the meteor shower was full of splinters

and the wind was green again, at the last minute, before it turned white

I begin using metaphors to try to tell people about what happens outside a doorway, those last seconds before silence. At the edge of a landscape, there is a mirage. When a person speaks, the mind invents a whole world. Hallucination is what we're already doing all the time. How can we create more moments that behave like thresholds? We should do this, because otherwise how can we know what it is to be ephemeral? Build doors and windows everywhere, or identify any given space as having the potential to be a doorway.

I lecture my friends about all this. They ignore my rants. I can't say directly what I mean because I'm caught up. Caught up in the system.

*

Outside the door, you spoke.

what's wrong with being swept away by beauty? all my innocent days

Inside, we drifted frictionless around each other in tighter and tighter circles.

Although I didn't speak, I made other sounds, and I heard myself moan before I heard it aloud. The moan became a solid frame, holding me in place. Within this system, the goal isn't to be in motion, but the opposite.

I carried the note until it became a part of the room, then the room carried it.

*

Eventually I was only able to talk about one thing: a particular plant, clustered purple spheres shining in the snow. Once I reached and touched them through a fog. How I thought of you. Metallic luster, little spheres, pearls. *Callicarpa*, beautyberry.

The system wasn't working as well anymore, the reflective surface, the pearls. We were each saying the same things over and over, then the door would slam shut. The trembling reemerged, but deeper, from inside the room or deep inside the body. But everything was fine, wasn't it? You just had snow in your eyes. *My beautyberry*.

*

It was October, the finest month. We drank whiskey in a purple room with low ceilings, and you touched my cheek in front of some people, which made me lose my nerve. As we approached the door, you said

things are simple and beautiful, and why not
when the world's a bit complex

I said

but lucidity about anything else

and I stammered, and the door shut behind us. The world here ends with a finality I savor, crave, crave, savor. Consequences don't announce themselves when the body's humming is so consistent (or so varied) nothing seems to be real, not even the body.

*

I now believe the silence
was pressed against us
from within the
room, from the other side of the
door, and before that door
ever opened, the silence began
to gesture in our direction
so forcefully it pushed
the unusual sense
of agency out
the backs of our heads.

Agency is conditional. This is why the things we said seemed to arrive from elsewhere.

Lists. Snowy roads outside the city, beyond where the buses stop, beyond the rows of beautyberries. Their purple glow. In powdered sugar, the imprint of your hand on my black dress, on the breast. Beautiful ideas, listening ideas. Statues, plaques. Doesn't everyone hide a lot though? Don't I hide too often behind statues?

*

I dreamed the bronze statue of the man in the town square had a cork in the bottom of his foot, and if you removed it, blood would soak out into the grass.

I kept bleeding out, as if I were a mammal constellation in the night sky, and you, a chart keeping time. White and red, the sheets blotted with blood. White and red,

red and white,

white, white, white.

*

A floating metal table and two folding chairs. A man I know is talking about devastation. I find myself saying it's sometimes responsible to hide one's devastation, but as I'm saying it, he looks at me harder and harder, until the words sound feeble.

The words fall out, click against the table.

The chairs orbit the table. At a different rate and through a different mechanism defined by the same principles, the table rotates on its axis. In general, the clouds are getting closer.

*

What happens within four walls. Or within anything, any constraint.

in the forest
no, on an island

on a forested island

The Moment can only lead to The Next Moment.

The Moment must be a set-up.

Your touch as you press me against a door: a step on the road toward the next removal. Each new distance becomes a reaching, a calling out.

Each calling out turns its chord toward a mirror and becomes a voice, embodied, four-dimensional.

And if the voice has a body, that body is something to relocate, something to place behind a statue or a door.

I had a body, I turned it
so it could hear better.

*

The problem spoke.
The problem was, the problem
said, then cut itself off.

In the grass, a row of metal boxes shone in the moonlight. But when we looked in one of them, the rainwater was gone. Each box had a little window on the bottom, a fine-mesh screen. The grass grew tall, wet, silver.

You said

all water was once ice, marbled

I said

and before that, the aqueducts filled the ancient pillars with helixes

*

I went to the woods

to feel the wind again.

The woods broke the sky into islands. Each sang of misfortunes and small gratitudes, which were sometimes the same. One rained with lines from a letter:

> *Do desire and fear create narrative, or is it the other way around?*
>
> *I'm plagued by these questions, but these questions also produce, for me, true moment-events: moments that lead only to themselves. So that 'time' and 'travel' are synonymous. I am alive.*

*

Today I woke up in a hotel bed beside you. Your voice fanning over me. Outside, someone was building a fire. The windows, flush with fire. When we touched, your skin didn't feel like anything but skin. Later, I sharpened my blue and purple pencils, I did an especially good job with the violence. Thin spiral husks fell on the sheets where you'd been.

ACKNOWLEDGMENTS & THANKS

Grateful acknowledgments to the editors of the following journals, in which versions of these poems first appeared, sometimes with different titles: *Colorado Review*; *Forklift, Ohio*; *Jellyfish*; *Quarterly West*; *Rockhurst Review*; *Sixth Finch*; *Sugar House Review*; and *Thermos*. Endless thanks to Christopher Janke, Heidi Reszies, Emily Hunerwadel, Jack Chelgren, and everyone at Slope Editions for making these poems into a bound object of the world.

I'm immensely indebted to Mary Jo Bang and Carl Phillips for their brilliance, kindness, and mentorship. Wondrous thanks also to Stephanie Dering, Niel Rosenthalis, James Scales, and Paige Webb, as well as the other writers who were in workshops with me at Washington University in St. Louis. Thank you to Tyler Duffy for time and friendship. Special thanks to francine j. harris, Dan Beachy-Quick, Claudia Rankine, Timothy Donnelly, Saskia Hamilton, Rick Kenney, Kevin Craft, James Arthur, Linda Bierds, David Wagoner, and Shaul Cohen, who at crucial moments gave me their time and attention, and who directed and sometimes redirected me. And thank you to Nancy Pope, the Olin Fellowship, and the English Department at WashU for generous support.

Thank you to everyone in my immediate and extended family, especially to Sheila Munsey, Genevieve Munsey, Robin Munsey, Lauren and Jamie Stephens, and Greg Heet for ongoing support and encouragement. And thank you to Kelly for unending enthusiasm and love, and for believing in my work.

I wouldn't be the person or the writer I am today without Rick Kenney's Creative Writing Seminar in Rome, which I attended in the summer of 2003. Thank you to dear friends and dazzling poets Laura Bylenok, Melissa Dickey, Zach Savich, Andy Stallings, and Jay Thompson, for being some of the best minds I've gotten to live among in language and life.

photo by William Youngblood

CASSIE DONISH is the author of *The Year of the Femme* (2019), selected by Brenda Shaughnessy as winner of the Iowa Poetry Prize, and *On the Mezzanine* (2019), selected by Maggie Nelson as winner of the Gold Line Press Chapbook Competition in nonfiction. Her poetry and prose have appeared in *Best New Poets*, *The Cincinnati Review*, *Colorado Review*, *Gettysburg Review*, *Kenyon Review Online*, *Tupelo Quarterly*, and elsewhere. She earned her MFA at Washington University in St. Louis, where she received an Olin Fellowship and served as the Junior Fellow in Poetry. She teaches at the University of Missouri in Columbia, where she's pursing a PhD in literature and creative writing. She grew up in South Pasadena, California.